Our Day in the Big City

By Jackie Tidey

Illustrations by Elizabeth Botté

Contents

Chapter 1

Planning Our Day Out

Dad said he would take Alice and me for a day out in the holidays. Alice and I like going to the city.

We looked on a **website** about things to do in the city. I saw that there was a new penguin show at the **aquarium**.

I printed out a map of the aquarium so we would know where to go.

See the
Penguins
MAP

After breakfast this morning, we helped Dad pack our lunch. Then, we walked quickly down to the end of our road to catch a **tram** into the city.

We didn't have long to wait, and soon we were on our way.

86
TIMETABLE

Chapter 2

Into the City

As the tram rattled along, we saw lots of people hurrying up and down the streets.

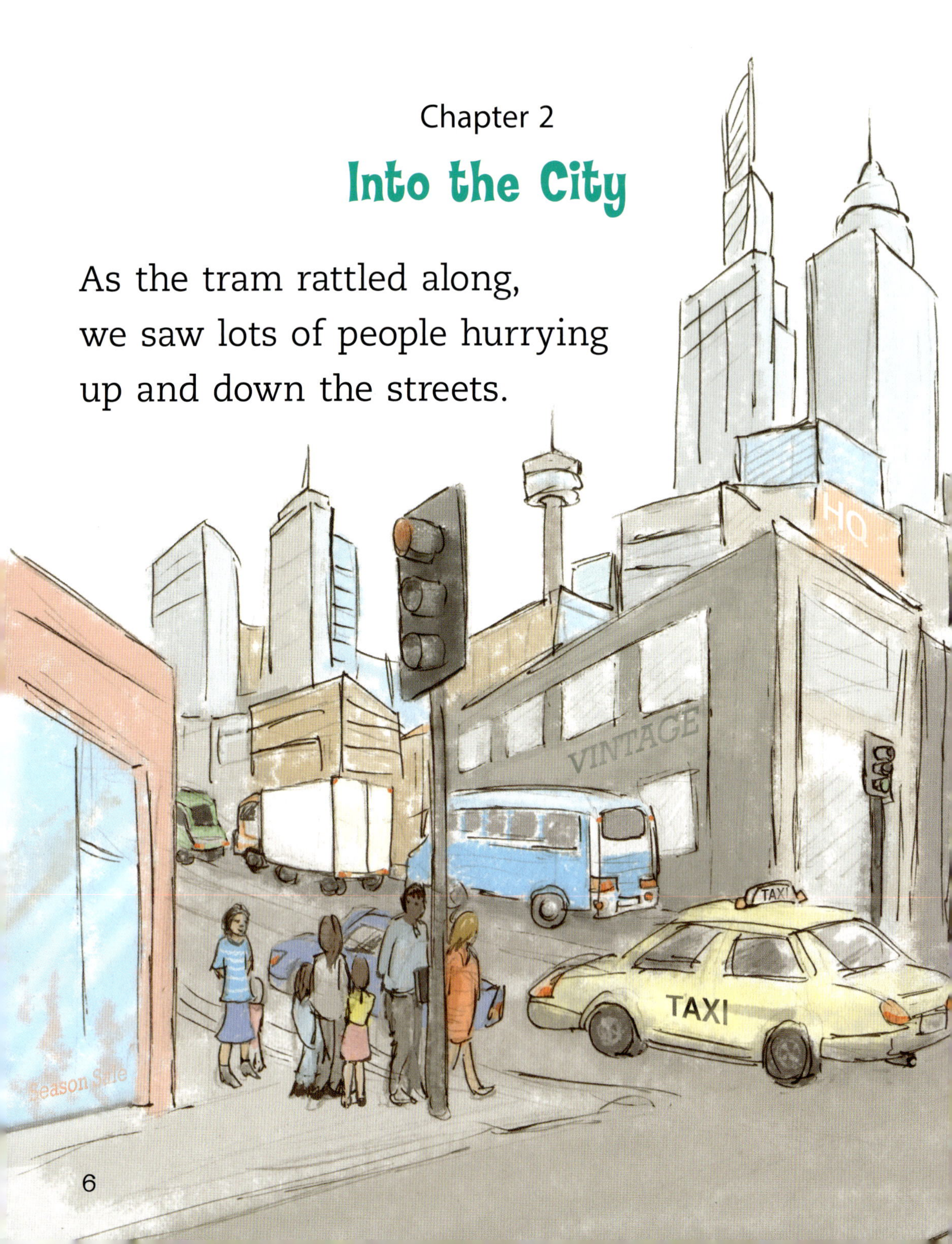

And we saw so many tall buildings
and cars and trucks and buses.

The city was very big and noisy.

When we got off the tram
in the middle of the city,
I held Alice's hand.
I didn't want her to get lost.

The aquarium wasn't far from the tram stop.

First, we went to see the penguins.
We had to hurry, because the show
was just about to start.

There was real snow
for the penguins to walk on,
and a pool with big blocks of ice.
The penguins kept trying to jump onto the ice.
Some of them went sliding off the ice
into the water.
The penguins looked so funny.

Chapter 3

Lunch by the River

After we had looked at other things in the aquarium, Dad said we could have lunch by the river.

Alice and I were glad, because we were getting very hungry.

We found a good place
where we could watch the boats going past.
One big boat had lots of people on it.
We waved to them,
and soon they were all waving to us.

Then, we went for a walk
and looked in the windows of the big shops.

Alice and Dad stopped to talk to a man
who was sitting outside one of the shops.
He was playing some drums.

Soon, more people came and stood near us.
The man began to sing quietly.
Dad put some money in a box
in front of the drums.

BOUTIQUE
No 15
HAIR
COCONUT

On the next street,
we saw a girl drawing a big picture
on the **footpath** with chalk.
The girl was very clever.
She mixed the colours
to make the picture look bright.

There were so many things to see in the city.

Then I saw Dad looking at his watch.
It was time to catch the tram home.

We were all very tired,
but we were very happy.

Glossary

aquarium a place to look at animals and water plants

footpath a path for people to walk on

tram a vehicle that moves on tracks

website a site on the internet